weblinks

You don't need a computer to use this book. But, for readers who do have access to the Internet, the book provides links to recommended websites which offer additional information and resources on the subject.

You will find weblinks boxes like this on some pages of the book.

weblinks

For more information about saving water, go to www.waylinks.co.uk/series/improving/water

waylinks.co.uk

To help you find the recommended websites easily and quickly, weblinks are provided on our own website, **waylinks.co.uk.** These take you straight to the relevant websites and save you typing in the Internet address yourself.

Internet safety

↗ Never give out personal details, which include: your name, address, school, telephone number, email address, password and mobile number.

↗ Do not respond to messages which make you feel uncomfortable – tell an adult.

↗ Do not arrange to meet in person someone you have met on the Internet.

↗ Never send your picture or anything else to an online friend without a parent's or teacher's permission.

↗ If you see anything that worries you, tell an adult.

A note to adults
Internet use by children should be supervised. We recommend that you install filtering software which blocks unsuitable material.

Website content

The weblinks for this book are checked and updated regularly. However, because of the nature of the Internet, the content of a website may change at any time, or a website may close down without notice. While the Publishers regret any inconvenience this may cause readers, they cannot be responsible for the content of any website other than their own.

HODDER
Wayland

IMPROVING OUR ENVIRONMENT

Saving Water

Dr Jen Green

HODDER
Wayland

An imprint of Hodder Children's Books

Titles in this series:
Air Pollution
Saving Energy
Saving Water
Waste & Recycling

For more information on this series and other Hodder Wayland titles, go to
www.hodderwayland.co.uk

Series editor: Victoria Brooker
Editor: Patience Coster
Designer: Fiona Webb
Artwork: Peter Bull

First published in 2005 by Hodder Wayland, an imprint of Hodder Children's Books
© Copyright Hodder Wayland 2005

British Library Cataloguing in Publication Data
Green, Jen
Saving water. – (Improving our environment)
1. Water conservation – Juvenile literature
2. Water consumption - Juvenile literature
I. Title
333.9'116
ISBN 0 7502 4600 6

333.9

Printed and bound in China

The Publishers would like to thank the following for permission to reproduce
their pictures: Angela Hampton Family Life Library 18; Ecoscene *title page*
(Melanie Peters), 5 (John Pitcher), 6 (Mike Whittle), 15 (Erik Schaffer), 23
(Nick Hawkes), 29 (Melanie Peters); Edward Parker 12; Frank Lane Picture Agency
9 (Chris Mattison), 11 (Alwyn Roberts), 13 (Martin Withers), 14 (Martin Withers);
Hodder Wayland Picture Library: 10 (Chris Fairclough), 16; NASA 4; Still Pictures 21
(Michel Gunther), 22 (Hartmut Schwarzbach), 24 (Ton Koene), 25 (Bojan Brecels),
26 (Pierre Gleizes), 27 (Ron Giling); Topham/Image Works 17, 28; Topham
Picturepoint 19 (Syracuse Newspaper/C. W. McKeen/The Image Works).
Cover picture: Waste Water Treatment Plant by Getty Images

Contents

Words in **bold like this**, or in *italic like this*, can be found in the glossary.

Precious water

All living things need water to survive. Humans, for example, cannot survive without fresh water for more than a few days. Yet many people waste precious water, or do not take enough care to keep it clean.

Oceans cover seven-tenths of the earth's surface. This makes the planet look blue when seen from space. ▼

Earth's water is present in oceans, lakes and rivers. It is also found frozen as ice in **glaciers**. Almost all of earth's water is salty. Less than three per cent of it is fresh water that we can use.

▲ **All living things need water to survive. In this photo, a spoonbill wades in a Florida swamp.**

Using water

People use water in all sorts of ways. They use it at home, for drinking, cooking and washing. They also use it in different industries, such as farming and transport, and for making energy. But factories, farms, homes and schools produce pollution that makes clean water dirty.

In **developed countries**, where water is plentiful, people often waste it. In many parts of the world people do not have enough water. Everyone can help to save water by using it carefully and reducing pollution.

TRY THIS!

Water inside you

Did you know that two-thirds of your body is made up of water? When you drink, your body **absorbs** some of the water. The rest passes out as sweat and urine. You also give off moisture as you breathe. Try breathing on to a cold mirror. See how the moisture in your breath forms a fine mist.

Fresh water

We usually think of water as a liquid, but it can also be a gas or a solid. There is water in the air and even in the ground under our feet.

When water is warmed by the sun or heated in a kettle, some of it escapes into the air as a gas called **water vapour**. When water is cooled below 0° C, it freezes solid and becomes ice. Two-thirds of the world's fresh water is frozen as ice, which covers the **polar regions** and high mountains. Of the rest, some is found in rivers, pools and marshes, but most is found in rocks underground.

Ice covers about one-tenth of the earth's surface, mostly in the polar regions. A thick layer of ice covers the frozen continent of Antarctica, shown here. ▼

Underground water

Some rocks are **porous**, which means they let water through, others are not. Underground water is found in moisture-soaked rocks called **aquifers**. When rain falls, it soaks into the ground and trickles down through tiny holes and cracks in porous rocks, such as chalk. When the water reaches a layer of non-porous rock, such as clay, it cannot pass through. The trapped water collects to form an aquifer.

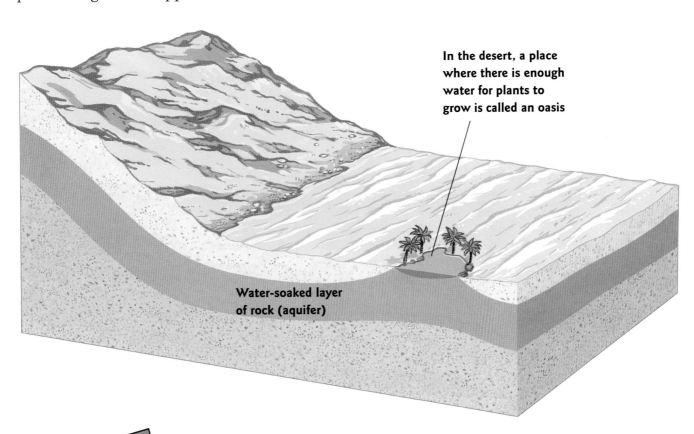

In the desert, a place where there is enough water for plants to grow is called an oasis

Water-soaked layer of rock (aquifer)

▲ Oases are found in deserts where water-soaked rocks lie near the surface of the ground.

TRY THIS!

Water near you

Is water plentiful where you live? In places where the rainfall is high, surface water often collects to form rivers, lakes and ponds. Dry areas have less surface water, and streams and rivers may only flow at certain times of the year. Find out more about water sources in your area by studying a local map.

weblinks

For more information about water sources go to www.waylinks.co.uk/series/ improving/water

The water cycle

Life-giving water circles constantly between the air, oceans and land. This endless journey is called the water cycle. Here's how it works.

When it rains, water soaks into the soil or drains away into streams and rivers. Rivers flow into the sea. Heat from the sun causes warm water to rise into the air in the form of water vapour. This process is called **evaporation**. High in the air, water vapour cools to form tiny droplets of water, which join together to make clouds. Later, clouds shed their rain, and so the cycle comes round again.

This diagram shows how water circulates in the environment. This process is known as the water cycle. ▼

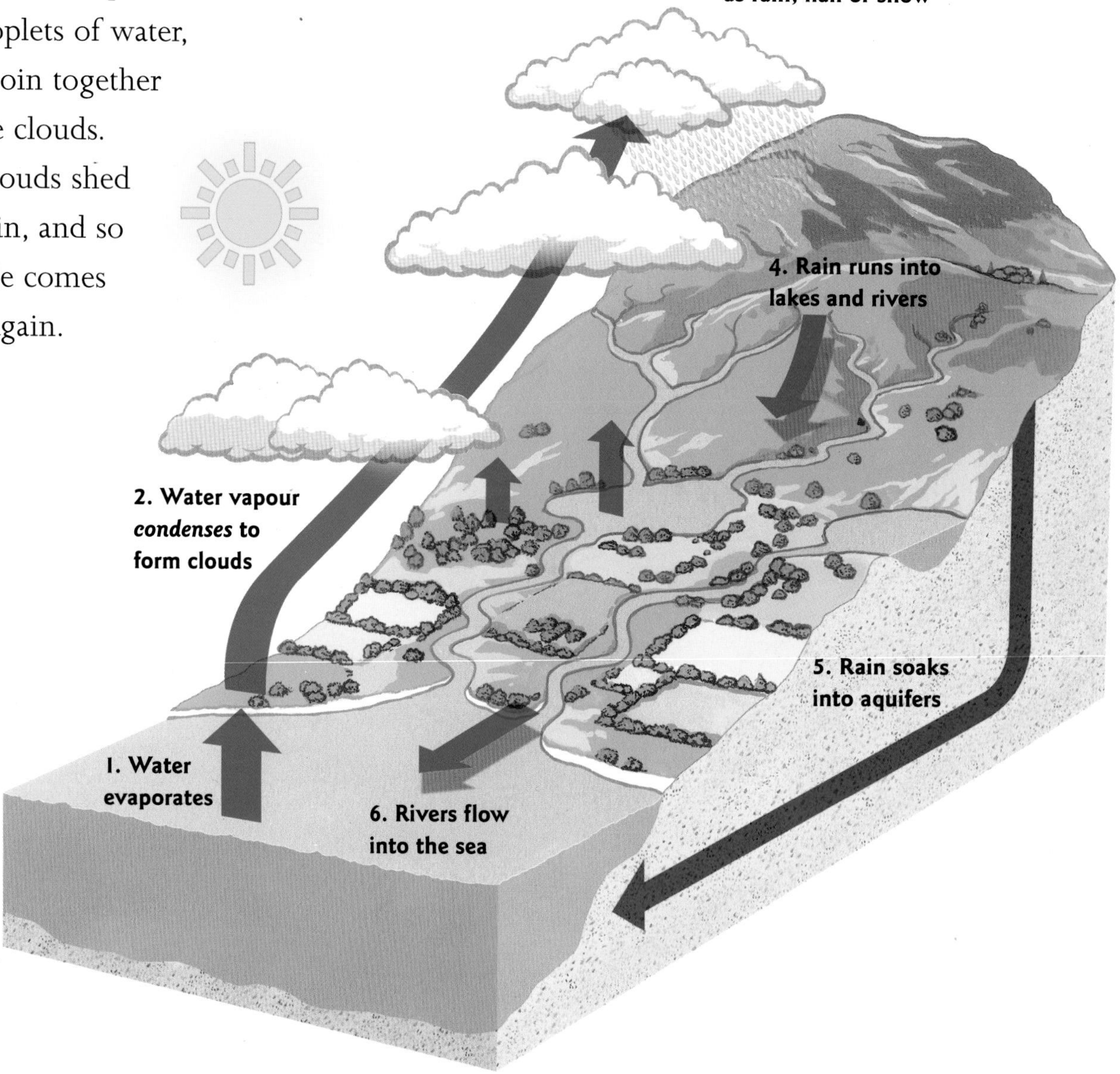

3. Moisture is released as rain, hail or snow

4. Rain runs into lakes and rivers

2. Water vapour *condenses* to form clouds

5. Rain soaks into aquifers

1. Water evaporates

6. Rivers flow into the sea

Rainforest cycles

Tropical **rainforests** are good places to see the water cycle in action. Rain falls there nearly every day. The trees absorb moisture through their roots and use it to grow. They give off excess moisture through their leaves. The moisture rises into the air to form clouds, which bring more rain.

Rain clouds gather over a tropical rainforest. The clouds are made from tiny water droplets that have formed when water vapour condenses. ▼

 TRY THIS!

Looking at evaporation

All plants give off water from their leaves, but you cannot usually see it. Try this experiment with a houseplant to see evaporation in action. Water the soil, then carefully place a clear plastic bag over the plant. Tape the edges of the bag to the pot. Moisture given off by the leaves forms a mist inside the bag.

💧 KNOW THE FACTS

WATER REVISITED
The water on earth never gets used up for good, but constantly circles. This means that the water you drink today is the same water the dinosaurs drank a hundred million years ago!

Daily needs

Although water never gets used up for good, it is not evenly distributed throughout the world.

In developed countries, water is usually plentiful. It gushes out of the tap whenever we need it. It is easy to take water for granted, but in many parts of the world water is scarce. In dry places, such as parts of Africa, people walk for hours every day just to fetch enough water for their family. In long, dry periods called **droughts**, plants, animals and people die of thirst.

In *developing countries*, many homes do not have running water. People fetch water from the local well or pump. ▼

Water for life

Experts say that everyone needs at least 50 litres of water a day for drinking, cooking and washing. Yet in dry parts of Africa, people survive on less than 10 litres of water a day. Meanwhile, in developed countries many people are careless with water. In Britain, most people use about 200 litres of water a day – four times more than is needed. In the USA, people use even more water – about 500 litres a day.

▲ In developed countries, many people waste water. Garden sprinklers make lawns lush and green, but use up a great deal of water.

HELPING OUT **Saving water**

Wherever you live, water is precious. Saving water is easy. Take a shower instead of a bath – showers are fun and only use about a third as much water. Turn off the tap while you clean your teeth, and rinse using a mug instead.

Water and the land

Water is vital for *agriculture*. Today, farmers use about 70 per cent of the world's fresh water supplies to moisten crops and water their animals. Water also shapes the earth's surface, creating *canyons*, cliffs, plains and valleys.

weblinks

For more information about irrigation go to www.waylinks.co.uk/series/improving/water

In ancient times people learned to channel water to grow crops. Certain crops, such as wheat and rice, soak up lots of water. Thirsty animals, such as cattle, use even more. In dry areas, farmers irrigate (wet) their crops using piped water or diverted river water. The amount of irrigated land has more than doubled in the last forty years.

In developed countries, such as Spain, many farmers use sprinklers for irrigation. Much of this water is wasted because it wets not just the crop but a wide area of ground, too. ▼

Shaping the land

The action of rushing streams, rivers and crashing waves shapes the surface of the land, carving out **gorges**, valleys, caves and cliffs. Where rivers meet the sea, they drop sand or mud to form a **delta**.

Stones and pebbles carried along by the river have helped to carve out the Grand Canyon (below) in the USA. ▼

TRY THIS!

Exploring erosion

You can find out how water wears away steep slopes by heaping up sand or soil to form a 'mountain'. Place stones or pebbles on the mountainside to represent rocks. Now slowly trickle water over the mountain. Watch the water rush downhill and carve **gullies** on the steep slopes. (Make sure you do this experiment outside, not in the kitchen!)

 KNOW THE FACTS

WATER INTO FOOD
The amount of water needed to produce one kilo of certain types of food is shown below.

Wheat	1,450 litres
Rice	3,450 litres
Beef	42,500 litres

Water at work

Factories use water to manufacture (make) many things, from cardboard to cranes and computers. However, factories also produce a lot of pollution that harms rivers, lakes and seas.

Factories use water in many different ways, for example, to wash, cool and drive machinery. Water is also used to transport goods, for example, to float logs downriver to the sawmill. Huge amounts of water are used in the **forging** of iron and steel, and in making paper and processing chemicals. Industries that use water for cooling often have tall towers that release clouds of steam.

Steam billows from the cooling towers of this power station in the UK. ▼

Pollution

The water spilling back into rivers from factories is sometimes heavily polluted, and it can poison water creatures. The factory water may be warmer than the river water, and this can also harm plants and animals. Factories, power stations and cars produce gases that mix with water vapour in the air to make a weak acid. When this falls as **acid rain**, it kills trees and plants and drains away to poison rivers and lakes.

◄ Rain containing weak sulfuric and nitric acid has killed these trees in Germany. The German word for acid rain is 'Waldsterben', which means 'forest death'.

TRY THIS!

Acid rain damage

In many areas, trees now show signs of acid rain damage, such as bare branches. Acid rain also eats away at stone statues, spoiling the carving. Can you see any signs of acid rain where you live?

Energy from water

People build dams on rivers and sometimes on coasts to make the most of the power of moving water. However, dams can harm the natural world.

This huge dam in Australia has a reservoir behind it. ▼

Damming a river helps to regulate the flow of water and increase its force, and thus the energy that can be generated from it. By channelling the energy of water rushing downhill from high ground, electricity can be produced. Electricity made in this way is called **hydroelectricity**. Modern hydroelectric power plants are often built below huge dams that hold back the water to create **reservoirs**. These artificial lakes store water for times when it is scarce.

Dams and nature

Unlike other energy sources, such as coal and oil, hydroelectric energy will not run out. The way in which it is produced causes little pollution. But large dams and reservoirs harm the natural world. When a new dam is planned, all the people in the area must move to make way for the reservoir behind the dam.

▲ The building of large dams like the Three Gorges Dam in China changes the landscape for many miles around.

HELPING OUT **Saving energy**

Dams and power stations are built to supply nearby cities with energy. But using too much energy is bad for the environment. We can all help by using less energy, for example by switching off lights and machines when they are not being used.

weblinks
For more information about dams go to www.waylinks.co.uk/series/improving/water

Water at home

Every day, we use large amounts of water in our homes. The dirty (waste) water we have used flows away down the drain and pollutes the natural world.

Modern kitchens contain machines, such as dishwashers, that use a lot of water. ▼

We use water in many kinds of ways at home – for drinking, cooking, and for washing our clothes, our dirty dishes and ourselves. We use water every time we flush the toilet or take a shower. Washing machines and dishwashers use a lot of water and many central heating systems contain water.

💧 **KNOW THE FACTS**

WASHED AWAY!
Below is a rough guide to the amounts of water used at home.

Cleaning teeth or washing face	5 litres
Flushing the toilet	12 litres
Taking a bath	120 litres
Taking a shower	15 litres per minute
Washing-up by hand	15 litres
Running the dishwasher	35 litres
Running the washing machine	200 litres

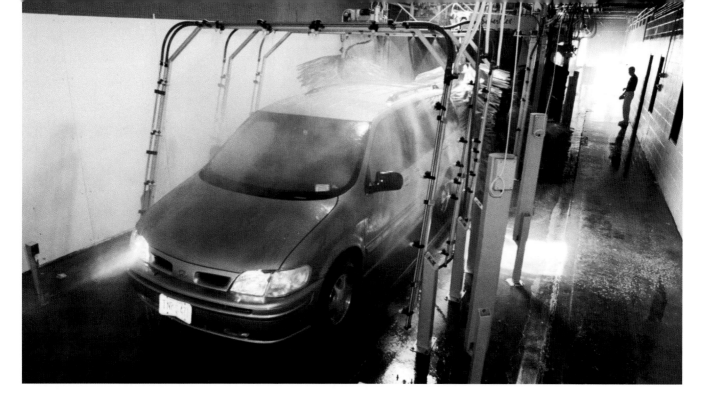

▲ **Automatic car washes like this one use more water than washing the car by hand.**

Waste water from homes

The water that gurgles away down the plughole is polluted by soap, washing-up liquid and other cleaning products. Water containing waste from toilets carries **bacteria** that can make people ill. These substances, called **pollutants**, must be got rid of in a way that makes sure they do not harm nature. Paint, paintbrush cleaner and oil from cars are all very poisonous and should never be poured down the drain. Your local council can tell you how to get rid of them.

TRY THIS!

Recording water use

Make a chart like the one shown here, listing all the ways your family uses water. Ask each member of your family to note down every time they use water over a weekend. Use the box opposite to work out how much water is used each time, and add up the totals. You may be surprised to find out how much water your family uses in just two days.

Water use in home	Number of times used
Washing/cleaning teeth	JHT ll
Boiling the kettle	lllll
Cooking	lll
Flushing the toilet	JHT JHT
Bath	l
Shower	lll
Washing-up	ll
Washing machine	ll

Clean water

In developed countries, the water flowing from the tap has been treated so that it is safe to drink. Waste water leaving our homes is treated again, so it does not harm water supplies.

Water drawn from rivers and reservoirs is pumped to a **treatment plant** to **purify** (clean) it. Firstly it flows through a grid, which removes twigs and litter. Then it passes through **settling tanks** and **filter beds**, which filter out harmful substances. **Chlorine gas** is pumped through the water to kill off any bacteria that are left, then the clean water is stored in tanks or towers. Houses, offices, schools and hospitals are all supplied with this clean, safe water.

Water treatment is a very complicated process. This picture shows, in a simple form, how untreated and waste water are purified. ▼

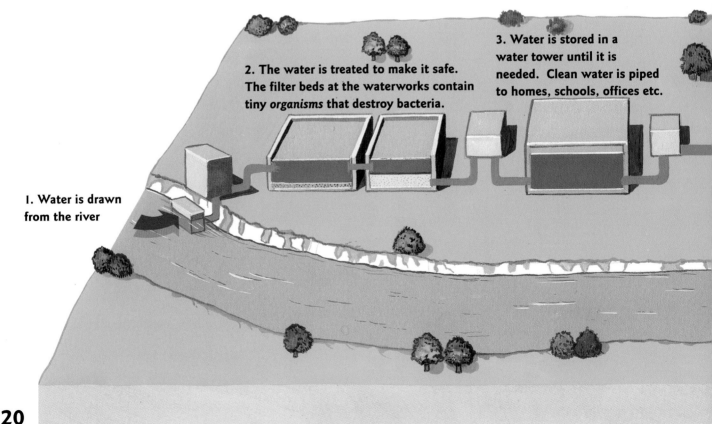

1. Water is drawn from the river

2. The water is treated to make it safe. The filter beds at the waterworks contain tiny *organisms* that destroy bacteria.

3. Water is stored in a water tower until it is needed. Clean water is piped to homes, schools, offices etc.

Sewage treatment

Dirty water containing human waste is treated at a **sewage** works before being returned to the river. Again, it passes through a grid and settling tanks to remove the solid matter (called sludge). **Micro-organisms** are added to work on the solid and liquid waste and destroy harmful bacteria. Finally the clean water drains off into rivers and streams.

▲ **At the sewage works, liquid waste is treated in circular tanks like these.**

TRY THIS!

Make a water filter

Make your own water filter using a funnel, cotton wool, blotting paper, sand and gravel. Stand the funnel in a jar and plug the neck of the funnel with cotton wool. Add a layer of gravel and sand, then blotting paper trimmed to fit on top. Pour muddy water into your filter and see how clean water trickles through into the jar. But beware – the filtered water still isn't safe to drink!

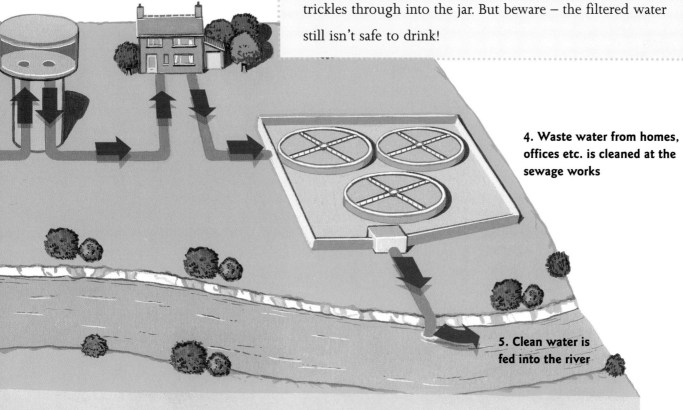

4. Waste water from homes, offices etc. is cleaned at the sewage works

5. Clean water is fed into the river

Dirty water

Many developing countries lack supplies of clean drinking water. Dirty water can make people ill. It can also cause tiny plants called *algae* to breed out of control, and these can damage the environment.

Experts estimate that up to a fifth of the world's population is without clean water. In developing countries, many lakes, rivers and streams are polluted by waste containing dangerous bacteria. After drinking dirty water, people can develop deadly diseases such as **cholera** and **typhoid**.

In India, much of the water in streams and rivers is polluted. People who use dirty river water for drinking and bathing may become ill. ▼

Pollution from farming

In developed countries, farmers use mineral **fertilizers** to improve the soil so that they can grow crops. When fertilizer drains off the land into rivers, it makes the water extra-rich in minerals. The algae multiply (breed quickly) to smother the surface, blocking out the light. They harm fish and other river life by using up all the **oxygen** in the water.

▲ Algae have bred to cover the surface of this canal in England with a green blanket.

TRY THIS! ## Signs of pollution

How clean are the rivers, lakes and ponds in your area? Look for these signs. If there is scum, oil or dead fish floating on the surface, you can tell that the water is polluted. Litter, such as plastic bags and bottles, spoils the look of many **wetlands**, and can also harm plants and animals.

When water is scarce

In dry areas of the earth, such as parts of Africa and the Middle East, water is always scarce because so little rain falls. Even areas where water is plentiful are sometimes hit by water shortages.

Life is a constant struggle in deserts and dry places. During droughts, the ground becomes cracked and dry, and crops wither. If **famine** hits the region, people may have to leave their homes to avoid starvation.

Life is hard when water is scarce. These children in Angola are fleeing drought, famine and also war. ▼

Saving water in dry regions

In dry coastal areas, a process called **desalination** is sometimes used to make fresh water. This process removes salt from seawater. However, desalination is expensive. Elsewhere, a method called **drip-feeding** may be used to irrigate crops. This involves laying a network of pipes to supply water direct to plant roots, instead of sprinkling it on the ground and wasting it. But drip-feeding pipe systems are expensive, too.

▲ In desalination plants like this one in Oman, water is heated until it evaporates. The water vapour then condenses as salt-free water. This is collected and stored in tanks or water towers.

weblinks

For more information about drought go to www.waylinks.co.uk/series/improving/water

Saving water, reducing pollution

Around the world, scientists, governments and campaigners are now working to reduce water pollution.

In recent years, environmental protest groups such as Greenpeace have helped people find out about water pollution. Many countries now have strict laws that prevent factories, farms and cities from polluting water sources. However, rivers and lakes are still polluted accidentally, and waste is still dumped at sea.

◄ **These Greenpeace supporters are protesting about polluted water from factories being released into a river in France.**

Demand for water

Every year, the number of people in the world increases and so does the number of factories. As a result, the world's water supplies are under increasing pressure to meet the demand. Experts estimate that the demand for water will rise by 40 per cent in the next twenty years.

▲ In Brazil, scientists take a sample of river water to check that it is clean.

HELPING OUT **Clean up!**

Litter in ponds and rivers can kill plants and animals. Birds and animals can cut themselves on glass and cans. They may choke on plastic bags, or get tangled in old fishing lines and drown. Ask your teacher if you can organize a school trip to clean out the local river or pond. Remember to wear gloves and always be careful near water.

Taking part

Everyone can help to save water and reduce the pollution that spoils rivers, lakes and oceans. If every family used even a little less water, it would make a difference to the world's water supplies.

Dripping taps waste a lot of water – ask your parents to fix them! You can reduce the amount of water used each time you flush the toilet by putting a weighted plastic bottle in the cistern. This will take up space, so less water is used each flush. Ask an adult to help. Washing dishes by hand, and only using the washing machine with a full load, also help to save water. Using a little less soap powder and washing-up liquid helps to reduce pollution.

A plastic bottle filled with water in the toilet cistern saves water each time you flush. ▼

◄ Save as much water as you can at home, then measure the amount of water your family uses in a weekend again (see page 19). How much water have you saved?

weblinks
For more information about saving water go to www.waylinks.co.uk/series/ improving/water

In the garden

Some families use a lot of water in the garden. A garden sprinkler uses about 800 litres of water an hour. Watering plants with a watering can instead of a hose saves a lot of water. Ask your parents to get a water butt (tub) to catch rainwater to water your garden.

HELPING OUT

Global warming

Recently the world's weather has become warmer and wilder. This is part of a process called **global warming**. Some dry parts of the world are getting even drier, and there is more risk of drought. Global warming is mainly caused by gases released as we burn fuel for energy and by vehicle exhaust fumes. We can all help to reduce global warming by using less energy and by not using our cars so much.

Glossary

absorbs takes in.

acid rain rain that is acidic because it is polluted by waste gases from factories, power stations and cars.

agriculture farming.

algae tiny plants that grow in water or damp places.

aquifer a water-soaked layer of rocks underground, that may feed a spring, stream or well.

bacteria tiny living things found everywhere on earth. Most bacteria are harmless but some cause disease.

canyon a deep, narrow, steep-sided valley.

chlorine gas a greenish gas, used in the manufacture of bleach and disinfectant.

cholera a disease spread by infected water supplies.

condense when water changes from a gas into a liquid.

delta a V-shaped area of land that forms at a river's mouth.

desalination a method of making fresh water from seawater by removing salt.

developed countries the richer countries of the world, whose industries are well-developed. Developed countries include the USA, Canada, many European countries, Australia and Japan.

developing countries the poorer nations of the world, whose industries are less well developed. Developing nations include many countries in Africa, Asia and South America.

drip-feeding a method of irrigating crops by supplying moisture to their roots.

drought a long period of time without rain.

evaporation when water changes from a liquid into a gas.

famine a major food shortage, often caused by drought.

fertilizer mineral food used by plants to grow.

filter bed a tank with a layer of sand or gravel through which water is passed to purify it.

forging shaping metal by heating and hammering.

glacier a slowly moving mass of ice found generally in the cold, mountainous regions of the world.

global warming a problem mainly caused by the burning of fuels such as coal, oil and gas. It results in warmer and wilder weather worldwide.

gorge a deep, narrow, steep-sided valley, often with a river flowing through it.

gullies channels or small valleys.

hydroelectricity electricity that is made by using the energy in moving water.

micro-organism a living thing so small it cannot be seen without a microscope.

organisms living things, including plants and animals.

oxygen a gas in the atmosphere, which animals need to breathe.

polar regions the regions surrounding the North and South poles.

pollutant any substance that causes pollution.

porous able to absorb water.

purify to clean water so that it is safe to drink.

rainforest a type of forest that grows where rain is plentiful.

reservoir an artificial lake used to store water.

settling tanks tanks in which solid waste settles to the bottom.

sewage dirty water from homes and factories, containing chemicals and human waste.

treatment plant a place where water is purified.

typhoid a disease caused by drinking dirty water or eating dirty food.

water vapour water in the air, in the form of a colourless gas.

wetland an area of fresh water, such as a stream, river, lake, marsh or pond.

Further information

Reading

Water (Interfacts series) by Brian Murphy (Two-Can Publishing, 1999)
Ocean Watch by Martin Bramwell/Blue Peter (Dorling Kindersley, 2001)
Our World: Water by Neil Morris (Belitha, 2002)
Saving Oceans and Wetlands by Jen Green (Belitha, 2004)
The Water Cycle by Theresa Greenaway (Hodder Wayland, 2000)
Geography First: Rivers by Nicola Edwards (Hodder Wayland, 2004)
Why Should I Save Water by Jen Green (Hodder Wayland, 2001)

Campaign Groups

Friends of the Earth
26-28 Underwood Street,
London N1 7JQ
Website: http://www.foe.co.uk

Greenpeace
Canonbury Villas,
London N1 2PN
Website: http://www.greenpeace.org

WWF-UK
Panda House,
Weyside Park,
Godalming,
Surrey GU7 1XR
Website: http://www.worldwildlife.org

Water Websites

http://www.unesco.org/water/wwap
World Water Assessment Programme

http://www.who.int/water_sanitation_health/index.htm
World Health Organization health and sanitation database

http://www.wcmc.org.uk
World Conservation Monitoring Centre

http://www.worldwater.org/
Database on world's fresh water

http://www.eia-international.org
Environmental Investigation Agency

http://www.mcsuk.org
Marine Conservation Society

Index

Numbers in **bold** refer to illustrations.